THE MILLENNIUM TREE
TAKETAKERAU

Marnie Anstis

Illustrated by **Patricia Howitt**

*If you don't know history,
you don't know anything.
You're a leaf that doesn't know
it's part of a tree.*

Sprawled on a rug in front of the wood-fire at Grandma's house, a child listened to Storytime on the radio. An elderly Maori gentleman – a kaumatua – was narrating a tale across the airwaves. The deep resonance of his voice was soothing, and with eyes half shut the child listened to the radio and drifted away with the story … away back into the past …

0 100 200 300 400 500 600 700 800 900 1000

Koro spoke:

Two thousand years ago on the far side of the world, a baby boy was born. He snuggled in his mother's arms, warm and sheltered in a stable. Cattle lowed softly in the hay while shepherds and kings laid down their gifts. In the vast black sky of twinkling stars, one bright, bright star beamed down a shaft of light.

> Silent night.
> Holy night.

Meanwhile — two thousand years ago, a berry germinated in a forest in a land in the south seas. The tiny seedling nestled under the canopy where shafts of sunlight beamed through branches and leaves. At night, the wind moaned softly through the bush. Stars twinkled in the vast black sky.

> Silent night.

| 0 | 100 | 200 | 300 | 400 | 500 | 600 | 700 | 800 | 900 | 1000 |

The seedling tree grew in an isolated land in a southern ocean — a green land set in blue, surrounded by a foam-white fringe scattered with flocks of seabirds.

It was a land of steaming volcanoes, boiling mud, and trembling earthquakes.

Grandma settled into her armchair by the fire alongside the child. She took a well-loved history book onto her knee and perched reading glasses on her nose. She brushed wisps of fine white hair from her brow. Grandma's bright blue eyes crinkled and her voice smiled when she read from the book. 'Listen to this,' she said to the child as she turned the pages.

2000 years ago Rome was the largest city in the world. It was a busy, bustling place, home to as many as one million people. Ancient Romans could go shopping and some children went to school. Using Greek and Latin — the languages of scholars — poems and biographies were written, as were books about history, politics, philosophy and science, on parchment scrolls made of fine, dried skin. The Romans traded goods with people from faraway places and paid gold for luxurious silks from China.

| 0 | 100 | 200 | 300 | 400 | 500 | 600 | 700 | 800 | 900 | 1000 |

It was a land where tall, dark trees towered over lush ferns, shrubs and vines that teemed with birds: stitchbirds and parakeets, saddlebacks and bellbirds, little wrens and robins.

It was a land where enormous eagles lived in mist-shrouded mountain ranges. With their huge wingspan, they could silently glide and swoop. With their vicious beaks and sharp talons, they could grasp and kill unsuspecting moa.

It was a land where busy streams and calm lakes sheltered ducks, swans and flightless geese.

It was an isolated land of wild beauty that no people ever saw.

Ancient Romans were talented engineers. They built apartment blocks four storeys high, and the city had sealed roads and traffic problems! The Romans built huge aqueducts to bring water from far away. Homes were centrally heated and had baths and toilets.

* * *

2000 years ago the Chinese traded goods with the people of Europe. Caravans of camels, piled high with colourful silk cloth, plodded thousands of kilometres along a dry, dusty trail known as the Silk Road, which linked Asia to Europe.

* * *

2000 years ago the Celts, who lived in Ireland, Britain and France, celebrated the harvesting of their crops on the last evening of summer. Druids, the Celtic priests, also lit bonfires to acknowledge the spirits and ghosts that they believed appeared on this last evening before winter. This celebration in autumn is the origin of Halloween.

* * *

2000 years ago Lake Waikaremoana in New Zealand gradually formed behind a gigantic landslip that had dammed a river valley in the rainforest 200 years earlier.

| 0 | 100 | 200 | 300 | 400 | 500 | 600 | 700 | 800 | 900 | 1000 |

The sapling grew within a jungle of trees among undergrowth of bushes and ferns, palms and vines. This verdant, tangled tapestry covered a sunny slope at the edge of the vast rainforest.

Soon the tree was big enough that kokako and pigeon could perch on the branches and survey the bush-cloaked, misty hills to the south. The roar of the sea was carried on the northerly wind which rustled the leaves. On a light easterly breeze came the sound of a rushing river.

Beyond the river were lowlands and swamp where bittern and kingfisher, stilts and moa, rail and weka foraged among bushes of manuka, raupo and flax.

In about the year 30 Jesus was put to death on a cross. His teachings formed the basis of a new religion — Christianity.

* * *

In the year 79 the massive eruption of Mt Vesuvius in Italy killed 2000 people when it buried the city of Pompeii under a layer of ash and pumice.

* * *

The Colosseum was a huge public arena in Rome where 50,000 people were entertained by gladiator battles — gory sword fights between men, to the death. Today, the remains of Roman architecture can still be seen in Europe — almost 2000 years after being built.

| 0 | 100 | 200 | 300 | 400 | 500 | 600 | 700 | 800 | 900 | 1000 |

Along with insects, these birds lived in a world that was their own. Except for small nocturnal bats and some lizards and frogs, there were no animals.

No animals … and no people.

The young tree grew in a place just beyond any catastrophic volcanic activity. It grew tall and strong as it reached for the sky.

China was a land of remarkable creativity. In the 1st century, the Chinese developed a new process — they discovered that by mixing different plant fibres with water, pressing the paste flat to squeeze out the fluid and drying the remaining pulp, they produced sheets of paper.

The Han Dynasty extended the ancient Great Wall of China further westward across the Gobi Desert, to help protect the Silk Road from attacks by nomads and bandits.

* * *

In about the year 200 a stupendous volcanic explosion formed a crater that became Lake Taupo. More than a hundred cubic kilometres of material were ejected. The landscape was utterly devastated for twenty kilometres all around and a layer of pumice covered the countryside for a hundred kilometres. Fine ash was thrown so high into the atmosphere that it circled the Earth. It may have caused the brilliant red sunsets recorded by the Romans and the Chinese vast distances away.

| 0 | 100 | 200 | 300 | 400 | 500 | 600 | 700 | 800 | 900 | 1000 |

Birds sang in its branches. The dawn chorus soared like a choir.

The clear, melodic notes, multiplied by hundreds and thousands of birds in the bush, created a resounding symphony every morning.

Their song gave rhythm to the days. The seasons gave rhythm to the years. And the centuries slowly rolled by.

Grandma flicked through the pages of her history book and read out bits and pieces that caught her attention …

Romans controlled 'Britannia' — now Great Britain — between the 1st and 4th centuries.

* * *

In the 3rd century the Chinese invented the compass and the wheelbarrow. In the 5th century they produced newspapers and printed books. They also invented gunpowder and made firecrackers for the first time!

* * *

In the 5th century the ferocious Attila the Hun led tribes from Central Asia on horseback, to attack and raid the people of Europe.

* * *

Around that time Anglo-Saxons from Germany invaded and settled the land we now call Britain. They gradually replaced the Celtic language with their own — now referred to as Olde English.

0   100   200   300   400   500   600   700   800   900   1000

The tree grew broad and handsome. Now around five hundred years old, it had a massive pale trunk covered with mosses and lichen.

Huia probed their long curved beaks into decaying wood in search of spiders and weta.

Piopio, the gentle thrush, nested in crevices in the trunk, low down and close to the ground — close to the sweet fuchsia berries.

Hihi, the stitchbird, built its nest high in the stout, spreading branches which grew up to the forest canopy where clusters of glossy, wrinkled, deep-green leaves glistened and reflected the sunlight.

The orderly lifestyles of the Roman Civilisation collapsed when people disregarded the rules of their society. The Roman Empire split in two.

The western half suffered invasions of Huns and Nomads, Barbarians and Vandals — tribes of nomadic, aggressive people from surrounding regions, who could neither read nor write. Books were burned. Buildings were neglected and towns deteriorated. Paved roads became rutted. Bartering — the swapping or trading of goods — replaced a money economy. This was the start of the Dark Ages.

Meanwhile the eastern half emerged as the grand Byzantine Empire. Ruled from the strategic port-city of Constantinople, the empire initially encircled most of the lands that bordered the Mediterranean Sea.

* * *

Around the world, many different calendar systems were used to record the passing of time. Then in the 6th century a scholar called Dennis the Short estimated the date of Christ's birth and used that as the starting point to calculate a new calendar, the Gregorian Calendar.

1100   1200   1300   1400   1500   1600   1700   1800   1900   2000

| 0 | 100 | 200 | 300 | 400 | 500 | 600 | 700 | 800 | 900 | 1000 |

Nestled among the leaves were small pink flowers, sweet and full of nectar — food for the songbirds that flitted in the treetops.

The flowers matured into red berries the size of marbles and were squabbled over by pigeons and parrots. Fantails chattered around the tree.

Early in the 7th century the Arab prophet Muhammad founded a new religion, Islam.

* * *

In the 7th century Mayan Indians lived in the jungles of Central America. Although their homes were in small farming villages, they built hundreds of temples, shrines and cities out of stone, where only priests and nobles could live. They wrote in books made from bark paper. Using their astrology and mathematical skills, they developed an accurate calendar and were able to predict eclipses. They built observatories to study the changing positions of the sun and moon, the planets and stars. But suddenly, the Mayan people disappeared. It is still a mystery as to why their empire vanished, leaving the cities, temples and shrines made of stone to slowly crumble beneath the encroaching jungle.

* * *

Fierce Vikings from Scandinavia invaded Britain in 793. Almost a hundred years later, Alfred the Great, an Anglo-Saxon king, finally defeated the Vikings — who were then granted permission to stay in Britain and settle peacefully in selected areas.

* * *

In the year 970 students were able to enrol at the world's first university, which still exists in Cairo, Egypt.

| 0 | 100 | 200 | 300 | 400 | 500 | 600 | 700 | 800 | 900 | 1000 |

As dusk settled, clouds of tiny bats were silhouetted against the sky. Laughing owls chased lizards and beetles. Moreporks silently devoured the huge lime-green ghost-moths that flew from the tree after dark.

Kiwi poked for grubs in the gloom of the undergrowth and pierced the silence with their shrill whistle.

Night came, then day.

The seasons passed by.

The years passed by.

The centuries passed by.

By the end of the first millennium, people had roamed and settled in lands around most of the world. China had been ruled by successive dynasties. The ancient religion of Buddhism had spread from India, through Asia as far as Japan. The Romans had ruled, and lost, vast areas of land all through Europe. Christianity had spread throughout Europe. The American continent was populated by American Indians in the north, the Mayan people in the central region and native American tribes in the south. Africans traded gold, ivory, spices and slaves to the wider world. Aborigines had lived in Australia ever since the Dreamtime — perhaps for as long as 40,000 years.

0 100 200 300 400 500 600 700 800 900 1000

Old trees died. Season by season, one by one, the gentle giants of the forest fell and rotted away.

Their place was taken by new generations of seedlings and saplings that sprouted from the forest floor and they too, in turn, became proud, tall trees reaching up to the canopy.

Why did this old tree live on and on?

By the year 1000, new farming techniques in Europe, such as crop rotation, resulted in more food and more people; more villages and more towns. This period is now called the early Middle Ages, or medieval times.

* * *

By now, Muslims had conquered the countries we now refer to as the Middle East with their new religion, Islam. The Crusades were an attempt by Christians, marching all the way from Europe, to regain control of lands that they valued too. The Crusades were a series of eight expeditions spread over two hundred years.

* * *

Around the year 1000, voyaging Vikings from cold northern Europe sailed across the Atlantic and landed on the north American continent.

* * *

Britain was in turmoil again. William the Conqueror from France defeated the Anglo-Saxons, winning the Battle of Hastings in 1066. This is now referred to as the Norman Conquest. William then ordered a survey of all British land, which was recorded in the Domesday Book. (Today, copies of this 1000-year-old book are in most libraries.)

| 0 | 100 | 200 | 300 | 400 | 500 | 600 | 700 | 800 | 900 | 1000 |

The tree had lived for a thousand years. With the ebb and flow of a thousand summers, it had welcomed and farewelled the migratory cuckoo. It had grown in a land that had only ever been shaped by forces of nature — ravaged by volcanic activity and howling storms, nurtured by warm sunshine and gentle rain.

The tree had grown in a land where, since the era of dinosaurs, the only *life* had ever been trees and plants, and birds and insects chirping in the sparkling sunlight.

It grew in a land where the only *sounds* had ever been the roar of the sea and the wind, the rumble of thunder and rain, and the cry of birds: the soft whistle of the huia; the clear melodies of the tui and bellbird; the haunting call of the kokako; the rich, low tones of the moa.

But this seclusion and isolation could not last forever. A new migrant was to arrive. Suddenly — and irrevocably — a new sound was to ring across the land: *the voice of man.*

About 1000 years ago Polynesian voyagers, while exploring the vast oceans around their warm island homes, discovered a new land to the south …

| 0 | 100 | 200 | 300 | 400 | 500 | 600 | 700 | 800 | 900 | 1000 |

Legends, myths and archaeology tell us that about a thousand years ago, large, ocean-going canoes made landfall on this lonely place in the southern seas.

The people who stepped ashore had brown skins and came from Polynesian Islands in the north, where it was warm all year round. Kiore (rats) and kuri (dogs) swam ashore too … Folklore has it that the people called this new land Aotearoa, the Land of the Long White Cloud. It was a cooler place.

Koro's voice was calm and gentle on the radio and the wisps and threads of the story floated and swirled around the sleepy child.

Until now, people in Europe had used cumbersome Roman numerals as a numbering system. Around the year 1100 the Arabic numbering system, which actually originated in India, was gradually introduced to Europe — along with a new concept called 'zero'.

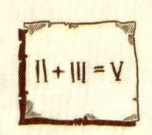

Grandma threw some more wood on the fire, which sparked, crackled and flared into life again. She studied the drowsy child at her feet, then turned the pages of her book and continued reading aloud.

Perhaps some giant eagles still existed when Aotearoa was first settled. Perhaps the eagles attacked people, thinking them to be a possible food source. Perhaps that was the origin of the Maori legend, Pouakai …

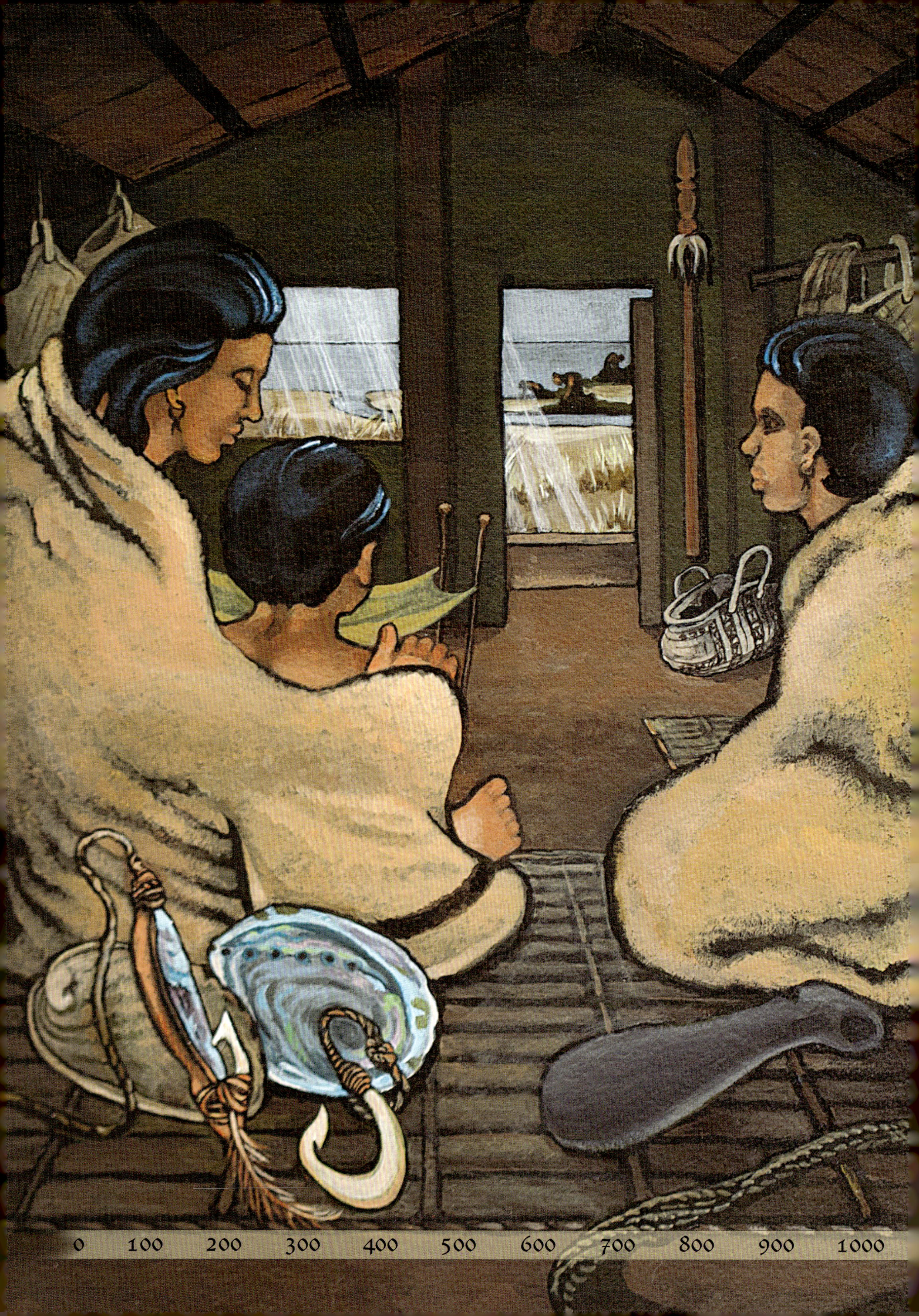
0 100 200 300 400 500 600 700 800 900 1000

The people lived on food gathered from the sea or along the shoreline. They ate pounded fern roots, which they harvested from sunny clearings. They collected berries in the seasons, and tender leaves from the bush.

These people adapted *to* their new environment using materials and resources *from* their new environment.

They caught eels from the swamps, moa from the lowlands and snared birds in woven traps.

They grouped into iwi (tribes). They built whare (houses) from the nikau palm and manuka, and lived in kainga (communities) with their whanau (families).

By burning the bush, they cleared land to grow crops of kumara, taro and yams. They fired hillsides to make it easier to hunt the moa.

The legendary figure of Robin Hood is depicted as having lived in Sherwood Forest in England in the 12th century.

* * *

Throughout Europe many magnificent Gothic-style cathedrals were built of stone: fine, tall and graceful, with colourful stained-glass windows. Famous examples include Notre Dame Cathedral in Paris, Westminster Abbey in London and Salisbury Cathedral in Southern England.

* * *

In England in 1215, King John signed the Magna Carta, or Great Charter. This is still regarded as having been an important advancement to ensure laws were fair for everyone, and justice was equal for all people. One of the original copies is still displayed in Salisbury Cathedral.

* * *

Marco Polo was a merchant from Venice who explored many routes and detours along the length of the Silk Road. Upon his return from China, he wrote a travelogue about the 'unknown, mysterious' lands of Asia. The story of his journey became a controversial bestseller in medieval Europe.

| 0 | 100 | 200 | 300 | 400 | 500 | 600 | 700 | 800 | 900 | 1000 |

And so they named the different types of trees and plants in the forests; the mighty rimu and totara, the tawa, tanekaha and the kohekohe.

But the trees with great pale trunks, glossy, wrinkled, deep-green leaves and flowers that turned into red berries, they called *puriri*.

During the late 1300s a new volcano in Aotearoa exploded through the surface of the sea, destroying nearby kainga. Today, the distinctive cone of Rangitoto in the Waitemata Harbour is a familiar Auckland landmark.

In the 14th century the ghastly Black Death, bubonic plague, raged throughout Europe. Carried by fleas and rats, the disease killed 25 million — about a third of the people who lived in Europe. This was one of the world's worst-ever disasters.

During the Hundred Years' War in the 14th century, the English practised target shooting with their newly developed longbow against the French, who used their new deadly crossbow design.

When the knowledge of gunpowder spread from China to Europe, the Hundred Years' War between France and England became even bloodier. Soldiers now used another powerful new Chinese invention — a weapon called a cannon.

| 0 | 100 | 200 | 300 | 400 | 500 | 600 | 700 | 800 | 900 | 1000 |

The people wove flax to make cloaks. To colour the flax they made a yellow dye from the pale bark of the puriri.

The water from boiled puriri leaves was used to treat cuts and sores.

And they used the heavy, dense puriri wood to make paddles, tools and weapons.

Joan of Arc united the people of France as she too fought against the invading English. In 1431 she was burned at the stake by the English, for the crime of heresy — having religious beliefs that were contrary to those of people in authority. She was 19 years old.

* * *

In Europe, most sailors at this time believed the world was flat. They were frightened to sail beyond the sight of land in case they fell over the edge!

* * *

Having ruled Eastern Europe for 1000 years, in 1453 the Byzantine Empire was defeated when the city of Constantinople in the centre of the Empire was captured by the Turks of the Ottoman Empire.

| 0 | 100 | 200 | 300 | 400 | 500 | 600 | 700 | 800 | 900 | 1000 |

The grand old puriri was now fourteen hundred years old.

The kereru (pigeons) that perched high in the spreading branches could now hear happy shrieks and cries of children drift on the evening air. They could now smell the smoke of cooking fires from the kainga of the lowlands. No one knows just when it was that these people came upon the magnificent, ancient tree growing deep in the bush.

How awesome and majestic it looked. It was more grand than any other puriri they had seen. They gave it a special name of its own — Taketakerau — which means 'old strong trunk to support many leaves'.

The late Middle Ages (1300–1490) was a stressful time in Europe. Climate change lowered crop production. The population dwindled because of starvation, plagues and war. However, these tough times eventually passed by …

… and led into the Renaissance, an exciting time in Europe (1300–1600). People debated and developed new ideas and philosophies on art, religion and science. Printing presses were set up throughout Europe and books were distributed. Stimulating new ideas were now able to reach many regions at the same time. This motivated ordinary people to learn how to read.

Such widespread distribution of knowledge in Europe had never ever happened before. In this period covering several centuries, civilisation changed immeasurably.

Paintings became more realistic during the Renaissance. Leonardo da Vinci painted the *Mona Lisa*. On the ceiling of the Sistine Chapel in Rome, Michelangelo portrayed God giving life to Adam. William Shakespeare wrote *Romeo and Juliet*.

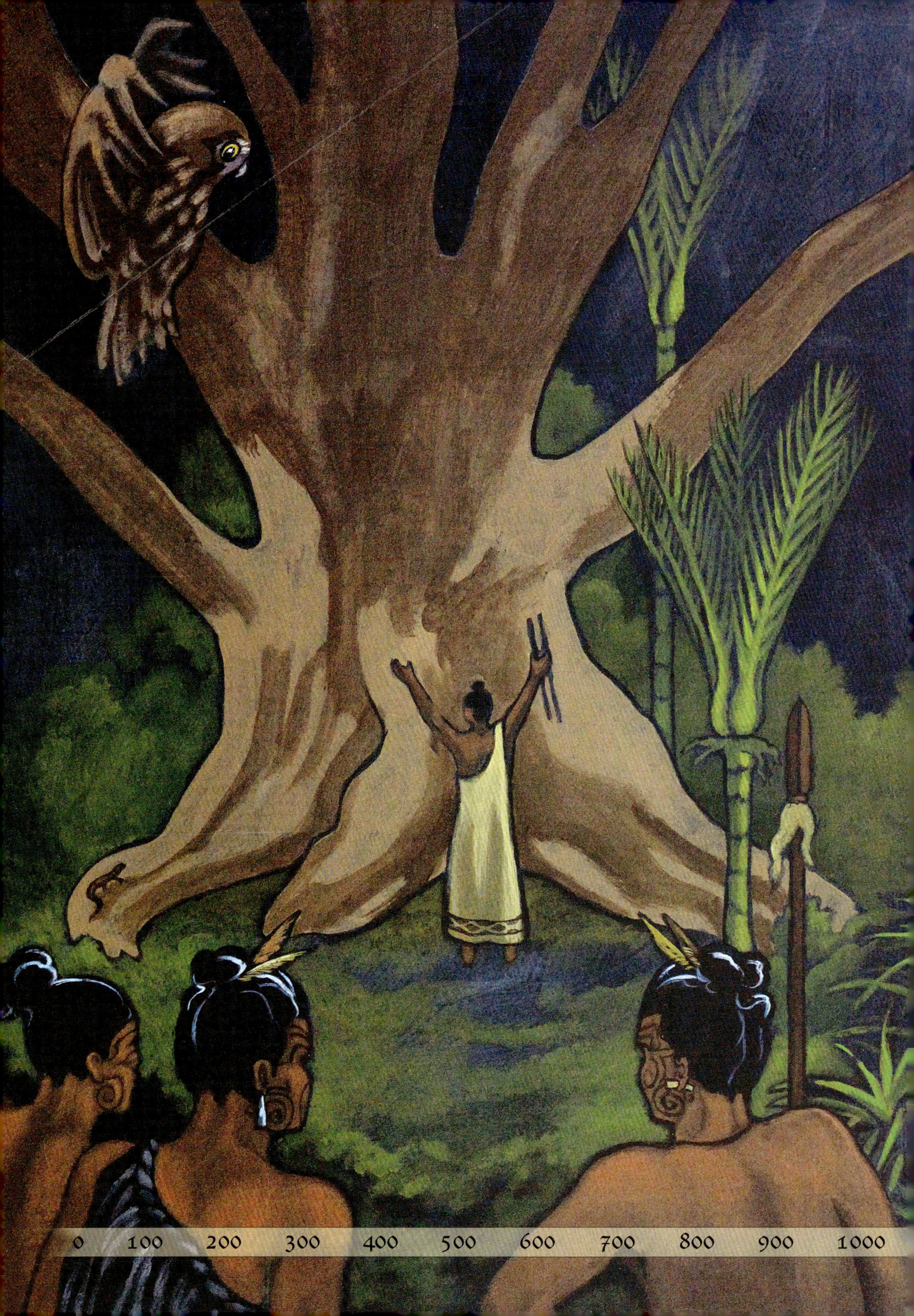
0 100 200 300 400 500 600 700 800 900 1000

The leaves shivered and shimmered in the breeze. At night, glow-worms softened the dark, shadowy grottos at the base of the tree.

These people placed a tapu upon Taketakerau: a fearful status befitting the powerful reverence and spirituality that the enormous old tree inspired.

Now the puriri was sacred and worthy of deep respect and awe. Now it was so mystic as to be feared! Now it could be used as a burial tree.

In 1492 a Spanish navigator, Christopher Columbus, sailed across the Atlantic Ocean and discovered the 'New World' — the Americas.

Did a Portuguese sailing ship make landfall in New Zealand in the 15th century? Some historians believe that it did …

* * *

In the 1500s Spanish conquistadors sailed from Europe and colonised the southern lands of the New World. They plundered gold from the Aztec people in Central America, now known as Mexico, and from Inca tribes that lived further south in lands now known as Peru. They brought with them the disease smallpox, which caused devastation within the local population.

* * *

During the 1500s the Ming Dynasty rebuilt sections of the Great Wall of China that had collapsed. At almost 8000 kilometres long, the wall is the largest construction on Earth. It is five times the length of New Zealand.

| 0 | 100 | 200 | 300 | 400 | 500 | 600 | 700 | 800 | 900 | 1000 |

Great importance was placed upon the burial rituals. The bones of their distinguished dead were laid in the ground.

After a period of time, the bones were dug up, scraped and painted with red clay to preserve them. Only then, with much ceremony, were the precious bones placed within the gloomy hollow that had formed inside the trunk, hidden in the darkness and shadows behind the ferns and undergrowth — hidden from their tribal enemies.

The years passed on. The centuries passed on. The moa and the huia passed on ...

Magellan was the first European to sail across the vast, calm ocean he named 'Peaceful Sea' — now called the Pacific Ocean. In 1522 he achieved another remarkable first: his expedition sailed right around the globe, thus proving the world was round like a ball, not flat like a tray.

* * *

The printing of many books had brought consistency to the different dialects of the English language. In 1604 the first Modern English dictionary was published.

* * *

While taking part in a protest against anti-Catholic laws, Guy Fawkes was caught with explosives as he hid in a cellar under the House of Lords in London, on 5 November 1605. He was arrested and hung for his part in the Gunpowder Plot — a plan to blow up the King of England and members of Parliament.

* * *

In 1620 the first white settlers from England, the Pilgrim Fathers, sailed to the New World on the *Mayflower* and colonised northern regions of America.

* * *

The oldest pukeko fossils found in New Zealand indicate these birds did not exist in New Zealand until the 1600s.

0   100   200   300   400   500   600   700   800   900   1000

Settlements of iwi (tribe) and hapu (sub-tribe) flourished along the coast and lowlands.

The bountiful region supported many hundreds of people.

Occasionally, marauding iwi clashed. Terrible battles were fought and much blood was shed.

The elaborate rituals at the burial tree took place many, many times …

Beginning in 1632, it took 20 years and 20,000 workmen to build the beautiful white-marble Taj Mahal mausoleum in India. Built by an Indian emperor in memory of his favourite wife, the Taj Mahal is set behind elaborate formal gardens. It now houses the intricately carved tombs of the emperor and his wife behind jewel-studded marble screens.

* * *

In 1642 the Dutch explorer Abel Tasman charted a short length of coastline in the South Pacific that was not known to people in Europe. The line was added to the map of the known world. This new mystery land was called Nova Zeelandia.

* * *

Already reeling from another epidemic of the plague, London faced a new disaster. In 1666 the Great Fire of London swept through the oldest part of the city, destroying the quaint wooden medieval dwellings within the walled section next to the River Thames.

* * *

For 400 years the (Islamic) Ottoman Empire had continually expanded the lands it controlled around the rim of the Mediterranean Sea and the Black Sea, with the city of Constantinople as its hub. In the late 1600s, the empire started a gradual decline until its eventual demise (in the early 20th century). Constantinople is now called Istanbul and is the largest city in Turkey.

| 1100 | 1200 | 1300 | 1400 | 1500 | 1600 | 1700 | 1800 | 1900 | 2000 |

0   100   200   300   400   500   600   700   800   900   1000

When Taketakerau was over seventeen hundred years old, the birds perched high in the branches may have looked over the treetops, past the river and out to the coastline.

Beyond the waves and towards the steaming island on the blue horizon, they may have seen the bright, white, square sails of the ship *Endeavour* …

When the sailing ship returned to its homeland on the far side of the world, word soon spread throughout Europe of new lands in the South Pacific.

Changes happened quickly now in the Land of the Long White Cloud.

In 1748 a peasant digging in his vineyard in southern Italy unearthed several marble statues. The discoveries led to the excavation of the lost Roman city Pompeii, which had lain buried and forgotten for 16 centuries since the eruption of Mt Vesuvius.

* * *

In 1760 Mozart was only six years old, yet he was already an accomplished performer and composer of music.

* * *

In 1769 young Nick Young shouted 'LAND!' from high up in the crow's-nest of Captain James Cook's ship, *Endeavour*. It took six months for Cook to chart the complete coastline of New Zealand. By 1770, New Zealand could be drawn on a map of the world. Botanists on the ship named and catalogued plants found on their voyage of discovery. Puriri was given the Latin name *Vitex lucens*.

* * *

In 1776 the American Revolution, also known as the War of Independence, occurred when the settlers of the New World fought against British soldiers to gain independence from the ruling monarchy of Britain. Following their victory, George Washington was elected the first president of this new nation, the United States of America.

* * *

A clock was invented that kept accurate time (based on Greenwich Mean Time) on a moving ship.

1100   1200   1300   1400   1500   1600   **1700**   1800   1900   2000

| 0 | 100 | 200 | 300 | 400 | 500 | 600 | 700 | 800 | 900 | 1000 |

People with fair skin wanted to live in this land too. They called it New Zealand.

Sealers arrived first — tough men to hunt and trade fur-seal skins.

Then sturdy whaling boats stopped by, spilling rough and rugged seamen onto shore, where they camped while waiting to hunt the whales that migrated along the coastline. Ship rats swam ashore too.

Marine chronometers became the foundation for great advancements in marine navigation and mapping, and the incidence of shipwrecks from navigational error decreased.

* * *

The king, the church and the noblemen controlled France during the late 1700s. Poor people, middle-class merchants and tradespeople were not represented in Parliament. The uprising by these people against the ruling classes is known as the French Revolution. Thousands of people were executed by being beheaded with the guillotine.

Following the French Revolution, Napoleon became Emperor of France. During his reign, he introduced basic rights in education, justice and politics for everyone. His influence is still apparent in the laws of many European countries. However, he is best remembered as a general, for his astounding military conquests throughout Europe, and for his defeat at the Battle of Waterloo in 1815.

James Watt's newly invented, reliable steam engine was incorporated into manufacturing industries throughout Europe and America in the early 1800s. This enabled many tedious jobs like spinning yarn or weaving cloth, that had always been done by hand, to be completed more quickly and efficiently by machines. Mechanisation drastically changed the way that people lived and worked. This period is known as the Industrial Revolution.

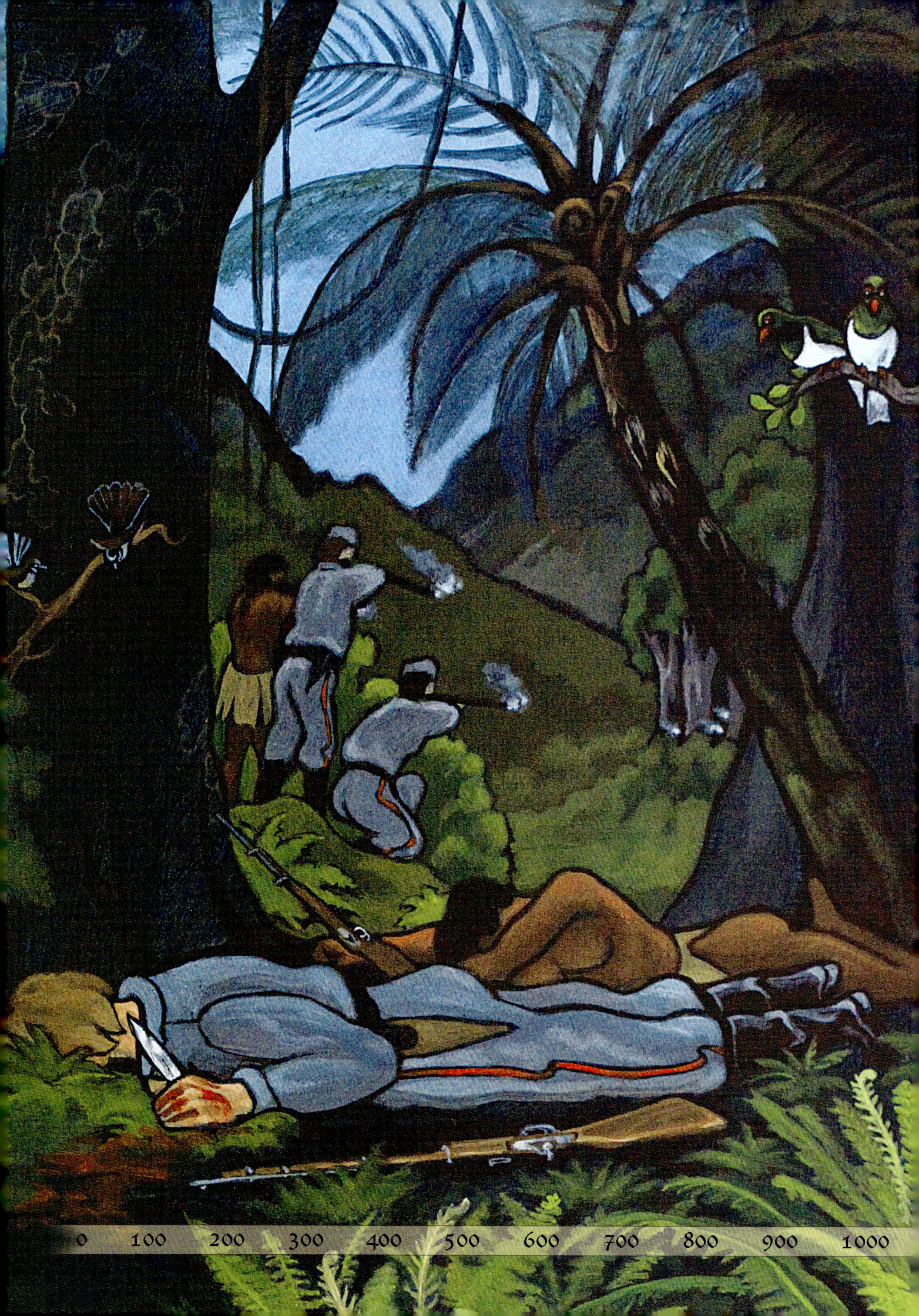
0
100
200
300
400
500
600
700
800
900
1000

Missionaries landed and preached Christianity.

Miners flocked to fresh goldfields in search of fortune.

Shiploads of settlers arrived from England and scattered across the land. These people *also* adapted to their new environment. In doing so, they disturbed the Maori way of life. There was a clash of cultures, and disputes over land erupted into fierce wars.

Again, new and different noises wafted on the breeze to where Taketakerau stood — the ring of the axe and the rasp of the saw; the dull, heavy thud as fallen puriri trees were split for fenceposts; the roar of fire and acrid smell of smoke as the felled bush was burned.

In the distance, horses and cattle and sheep could be heard calling in the still air of morning. They needed grass to eat. And so did lots of rabbits …

The first attempt to write the spoken Maori language was made by missionaries when they arrived in New Zealand. Several years later, Professor Samuel Lee of Cambridge University in England, assisted by a northern Maori leader Hongi Hika, devised a formal written structure of the Maori language and compiled the first Maori dictionary. By the mid-1820s, the Maori language was able to be written and read.

* * *

Following skirmishes with rival chiefs, Shaka became leader of the Zulu tribe in Africa. During his reign, he introduced sophisticated battle strategies, and exceptionally strict control which eventually encompassed 250,000 tribal people to form the Zulu Kingdom.

* * *

New Zealand established trading links with the rest of the world. Wool was first exported from New Zealand in 1835. Ten years later, the first shipment of butter and cheese sailed to Sydney.

* * *

Dr David Livingstone, the missionary and explorer, endured harsh conditions during his exploration of Africa in the 1800s. His optimistic attitude — 'I am prepared to go anywhere, provided it be forward' — enabled him to overcome huge obstacles in his quest to find the source of the Nile. The longest river in the world, the Nile flows 6500 kilometres — from south of the equator in the Great Lakes region of central Africa, northwards to spill into the Mediterranean Sea, well beyond the Tropic of Cancer.

1100 1200 1300 1400 1500 1600 1700 **1800** 1900 2000

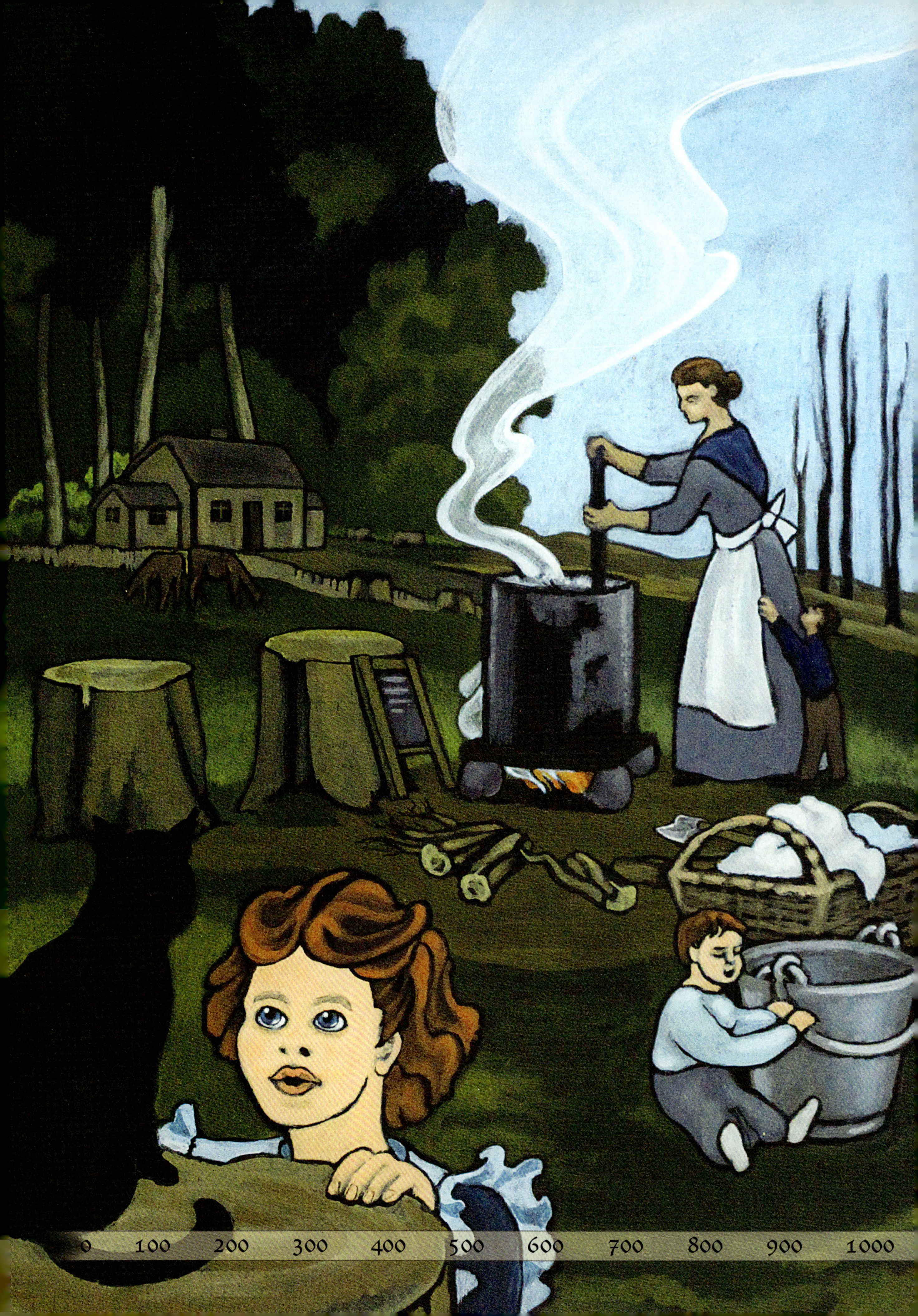
0 100 200 300 400 500 600 700 800 900 1000

The vast areas of bush were gone.

The trees that towered over lush ferns and shrubs and vines were gone.

Weasels and stoats were released to control the rabbits. The gentle little thrush, piopio, disappeared. The laughing owl was heard no more.

The few songbirds left in the remnants of bush were not enough to create a soaring concerto each morning — only a chorus.

For several years, New Zealand was under the jurisdiction of the governor of New South Wales in Australia. Then, in 1840, British Sovereignty was proclaimed in New Zealand. The Treaty of Waitangi was signed. The treaty was an agreement between representatives of the British government and Maori chiefs, representing their tribes.

Captain William Hobson was the first governor of New Zealand.

* * *

The first Maori language newspaper was published in 1842.

* * *

Fleeing Ireland during the Potato Famine in the 1840s, Irish immigrants brought the ancient Celtic custom of Halloween to their new homeland, the United States of America.

* * *

In 1855 Wellington experienced the most powerful earthquake ever recorded in New Zealand. It was 8.2 in magnitude.

In 1856 Christchurch was the first town in New Zealand to be officially deemed a city.

Originally established in the Bay of Islands, then moved to Auckland, the capital of New Zealand was eventually shifted to Wellington in 1865.

* * *

Abraham Lincoln was president of the United States during the American Civil War of the 1860s. The five-year battle to end slavery was fought between the northern and southern states.

0	100	200	300	400	500	600	700	800	900	1000

When dustings of fine grey volcanic ash settled on its leaves, Taketakerau looked old. Taketakerau was old.

Taketakerau was ancient. Taketakerau was over nineteen hundred years old.

In 1868 New Zealand became the first country in the world to allow its native people to vote. Twenty-five years later New Zealand also became the first country to allow women to vote.

* * *

Communication methods were getting faster and faster. Telegraph lines were strung from town to town and telegraph cables were laid under the sea — across Cook Strait in 1866, and from New Zealand to Australia in 1876.

The invention of refrigeration was important to the development and wealth of New Zealand. Being able to export frozen meat to England by sea opened up valuable and exciting new markets and opportunities. The first consignment left Dunedin — on the sailing ship *Dunedin* — in 1882.

Transportation methods were getting faster too. Steam ships replaced sailing ships. Trains were developed to pull coaches of passengers. People learned to fly in amazing new flying machines.

* * *

Coca Cola was concocted in Atlanta, USA, in 1886.

* * *

Mt Tarawera unexpectedly erupted in 1886. The four hours of volcanic devastation created a five kilometre chasm along the top of the mountain, buried two villages at its base and killed 150 people. A world-famous tourist attraction, the Pink and White Terraces were lost under mud and debris.

0   100   200   300   400   500   600   700   800   900   1000

The sacred, secret, gnarled old puriri tree was still sheltered from civilisation, deep within a small stand of native bush. Only the Maori people, the people of the Upokorehe hapu,* knew of its existence.

But the seasons and the years and the centuries were taking their toll.

A fierce thunderstorm in 1913 ripped off a massive branch, which crashed to the ground flattening ferns and undergrowth.

A settler out searching deep in the bush for his lost horse suddenly came upon the huge old puriri tree — the wrenched branch lying at its foot, the wounded trunk oozing sap. And there, exposed in the fresh gash of the hollow trunk, open to the light, open to view, open for all to see, were the sacred bones of Maori …

* A sub-tribe of Whakatohea, the predominant Maori tribe of the locality.

It took until the turn of the 20th century for the Gregorian Calendar to be widely accepted for international use. This is the calendar system used in New Zealand. However, there are many other different calendars still in use throughout the world today, such as the Islamic, Hindu and Chinese calendars.

* * *

In 1904, radio time signals (pips) were first broadcast directly to boats at sea. Knowing the precise time of the day enabled navigators to calculate how far through the earth's daily 360° rotation they were. This determined their longitude. Latitude was found by measuring the highest angle of the sun above the horizon. These two precise co-ordinates plotted their position on a chart.

* * *

The first All Black rugby team toured Britain in 1905.

* * *

On 9 September 1907 King Edward VII granted New Zealand the status of Dominion — an independent, self-governing nation.

* * *

In Detroit, USA the Model T Ford motor car rolled off the first mass-production assembly line in 1908.

* * *

In 1912, on its maiden voyage, the supposedly unsinkable luxury passenger liner *Titanic* hit an iceberg — and sank.

0   100   200   300   400   500   600   700   800   900   1000

News of the discovery of the enormous old burial tree spread quickly throughout the community.

The mana and mystique of Taketakerau captured the imagination and curiosity of many people. They wanted to see it.

To enable the tree to be accessible to everyone, Maori and Pakeha, the bones from the burial site were removed and re-buried with due ceremony.

The tapu was lifted from the tree and the fine stand of native bush was protected as a public domain and opened for all.

New Zealanders joined the rest of the world and fought in two World Wars — the conflicts were between the ideals of enforced control and democracy.

During World War I, almost 3000 New Zealand soldiers lost their lives in the 1915 Gallipoli Campaign in Turkey. The heavy losses from this disastrous battle fostered a national grief that united all New Zealanders — Maori and Pakeha — and memorial ceremonies have been held on 25 April ever since. Anzac Day honours all New Zealand and Australian soldiers who died in wartime while defending and guarding our free lands 'from the shafts of strife and war'.

* * *

In 1918 the Spanish Influenza epidemic is estimated to have killed 50–100 million people worldwide. In two months, over 8000 people died in New Zealand.

* * *

The development of electricity was applied to innovative audio devices — the phonograph and the gramophone record. Stimulating new sounds and fresh musical styles were now able to reach many people at the same time via jukeboxes and 'the wireless' — radio. Such widespread simultaneous distribution of the latest music had never ever happened before. Pop music arrived!

0   100   200   300   400   500   600   700   800   900   1000

Now everyone could marvel at this revered tree. Now everyone could gather at this ancient puriri with its massive girth and branches the size of other trees!

Now everyone could see where centuries of erosion had exposed the roots to create dark, mysterious, shadowy grottos within the trunk, behind the ferns and undergrowth.

For over 500 years, the British Empire had steadily expanded its rule over various territories and dominions to become the largest empire in the history of the world. At the peak of its power in 1922 it was in command of a quarter of the world's population.

Between the two world wars, the economies of many industrialised countries collapsed. Production rapidly declined and there was a sudden rise in unemployment. Around the world, millions of people lost their jobs, their businesses and their savings. Because they no longer had any money, some people had to walk out and abandon their homes. This period is called the Great Depression, and lasted for about twelve years.

* * *

In 1931 the cities of Napier and Hastings were destroyed in a powerful earthquake that killed over 250 people.

* * *

In 1938 the New Zealand government introduced the Social Security Act. This Act stated that every person had a right to a reasonable standard of living, and introduced the benefit system.

* * *

During World War II, Hitler's Nazi regime exterminated over six million Jewish people in Europe, mainly in deadly gas chambers. This is now known as the Holocaust.

0   100   200   300   400   500   600   700   800   900   1000

And Taketakerau *still* lives!

It stands in a fragment of bush near the northern fringes of the great Urewera National Park.

The roar of the blue Pacific Ocean is still carried on the northerly wind that ruffles its leaves.

The wood pigeons still perch on the high branches and survey the open farmland beyond the Waioeka River.

World War II ended soon after the invention of a ghastly new weapon … atomic bombs were dropped on the Japanese cities of Hiroshima and Nagasaki, killing 200,000 people.

In the closing stages of World War II in 1945, fifty nations signed a charter to form the United Nations — an international organisation for preserving world peace.

Following World War II, Britain couldn't afford to sustain its far-flung empire, and independence was granted to most of its territories and colonies.

* * *

For the average family in New Zealand, living conditions dramatically improved as plumbing systems (running water, drainage and toilets) and electricity were installed into homes.

* * *

From the end of World War II until the mid-1990s, tensions increased between democratic and communist nations. However, in spite of threats and hostilities, no direct military battle ever occurred. This 50-year period of mistrust and suspicion between the superpowers, America and the Soviet Union (Russia), is known as the Cold War.

* * *

In 1958 both Russia and America launched exploratory satellites into space. In 1969 astronauts Neil Armstrong and Edwin Aldrin walked on the moon. Many people were able to watch this incredible event at home on their television sets — as it was actually happening.

0   100   200   300   400   500   600   700   800   900   1000

Different noises now disturb the serenity. Farm tractors grind, home stereos thump, trucks rumble along the distant highway. The swish of speeding cars ... the swoop of top-dressing planes ... squealing kids that spill from the school bus.

Now blackbirds and sparrows chirp in flower gardens.

Now the evenings are disturbed by the harsh screech of possums.

But the clear notes of the bellbird still chime high among the flowers that nestle in the rustling leaves of Taketakerau.

Tui still squabble over the bright red berries. Fantails still chatter overhead. At night, the wind still moans softly through the surrounding bush. Moreporks still quietly devour the huge lime-green puriri moths. And sometimes, kiwi still pierce the evening silence with their shrill whistle.

At various times since the early 1900s New Zealand has been responsible for several island groups of the South Pacific — the Cook Islands, Niue, Tokelau and part of Samoa. Many Pacific Islanders regard New Zealand as a desirable place to live, and have formed strong communities in the larger cities.

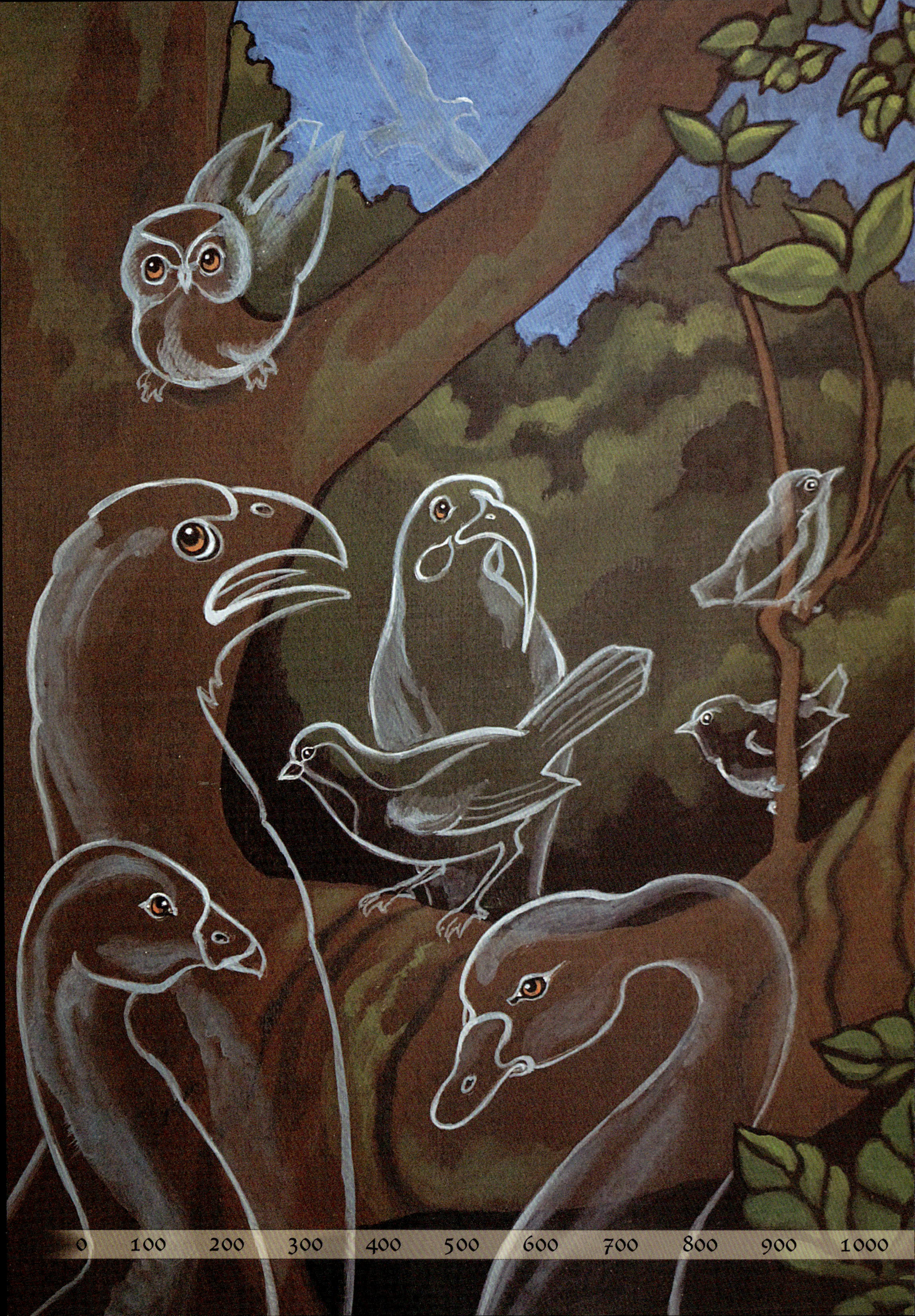
0 100 200 300 400 500 600 700 800 900 1000

This awe-inspiring puriri tree has lived in our land alongside many bird species that no longer exist — the giant New Zealand eagle, the New Zealand goose and swan, many species of duck, many species of moa, the piopio, the laughing owl, and the huia. All are now extinct.

Taketakerau has lived in our world since the birth of Jesus and the beginning of Christianity.

The tree is older than the Colosseum, older than Lake Taupo.

During the summer of 2010/11 Christchurch was rocked by a series of earthquakes. A major tremor on 22 February killed almost 200 people and seriously injured many others. Treasured heritage buildings within the central city were destroyed and almost 10,000 homes were damaged beyond repair.

People throughout the world were able to watch raw, unedited video coverage of the chaotic hours following the disastrous quake on their mobile devices, or at home on their television sets — as it was actually happening.

The death, injuries and destruction from this earthquake fostered a national grief that united all New Zealanders and prompted immediate international assistance.

| 0 | 100 | 200 | 300 | 400 | 500 | 600 | 700 | 800 | 900 | 1000 |

This gaunt, twisted, ancient tree has endured storms and gales, volcanoes, droughts and cyclones.

Taketakerau has lived through many periods of change — changes that often have been inevitable.

It has survived times of pandemic and of rebellion, times of conflict and of war.

Today people throughout the world can go shopping anywhere, using the Internet. People still write poetry and biographies. In a massive worldwide outburst of self-expression, they also write about history, politics, philosophy, science — and participate in interactive blogs and chitchat — on their home computers, laptops or mobile devices.

Nowadays, we are part of a new revolution, an 'information technology' revolution. Computers and the Internet have allowed ordinary people to find out information about anything. Such widespread, instant access to knowledge by people throughout the world has never ever happened before. In this period covering several decades, civilisation has changed immeasurably.

Grandma looked over her glasses at the child and laughed. 'But children still have to go to school!'

0   100   200   300   400   500   600   700   800   900   1000

Taketakerau has grown taller through times of discovery, of development and of progress.

Today, this extraordinary old tree, now estimated to be over two thousand years old, is a remarkable link between the past and the present. It is a living symbol of the third millennium, the era to which we now belong.

Taketakerau has a strong, sturdy trunk to support many leaves, and its longevity, fortitude and resilience can inspire us as we look to our future.

In the 21st century Auckland is the largest city in New Zealand. It is a busy, bustling city of more than a million people. It has sealed roads and traffic problems. It has office blocks that soar over 40 storeys high!

Today New Zealand's population is made up of a varied collection of people from numerous cultures and different ethnic groups — people who are adapting *to* their new environment using materials and resources *from* their new environment, and *all* of us have, at some stage, migrated and crossed over the foam-white fringe that surrounds our land … Maori, European, Polynesian, Asian, Indian, Middle-Eastern, African, Scandinavian …

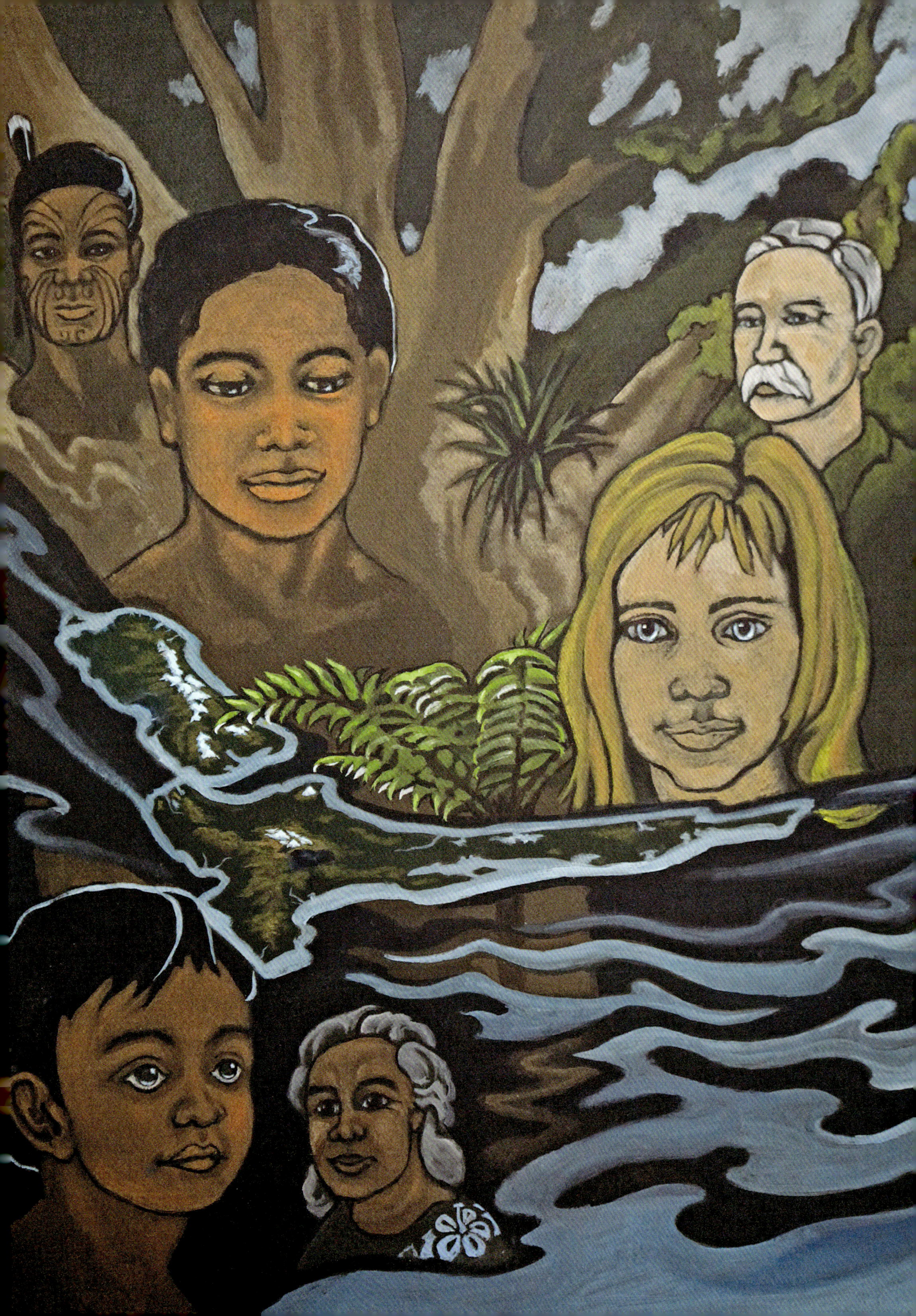

Koro finished reading his story.

The radio played the second verse of New Zealand's national anthem:

Ona mano tangata	Men of every creed and race
Kiri whero, kiri ma,	Gather here before Thy face,
Iwi Maori Pakeha	Asking Thee to bless this place,
Rupeke katoa,	God defend our Free Land.
Nei ka tono ko nga he	From dissension, envy, hate,
Mau e whakaahu ke,	And corruption guard our State,
Kia ora marire	Make our country good and great,
Aotearoa	God defend New Zealand.

Grandma closed her book. The child stirred and turned off the radio. In the silence, they heard the soft evening wind moan around the cottage. As the day faded, they sat together by the hearth and watched the glowing embers, lost in thought.

Silent night.

STORYTELLER: In this illustration, Koro's korowai (cloak), woven from flax fibre, is symbolic of the patterns sometimes used to record the stories of genealogy, history and legend featured within the woven designs on tukutuku panels and taniko borders. ▪ **Tui**, *Prosthemadera novaeseelandiae*

SILENT NIGHT: The **laughing owl**, whekau, *Sceloglaux albifacies* had a call that sounded like maniacal laughter. After surviving for an estimated one million years in New Zealand, it is now believed to be extinct. ▪ The **giant snail**, ngata, puturangi, of the species *Powelliphanta* is a nocturnal meat-eater that slurps on earthworms and slugs. This endangered gastropod is able to live for up to 20 years and grow to the size of a man's fist. ▪ **Huhu beetle** (flying), tunga rere, *Prionoplus reticularis* ▪ **Puriri** berry and seedling, *Vitex lucens* ▪ **Nikau palm** *Rhopalostylis sapida* ▪ The stems of the flowers of NZ Mahogany, **kohekohe**, *Dysoxylum spectabile* sprout directly out of the tree-trunk. ▪ **Supplejack vine**, kareao, *Ripogonum scandens*

FOAM-WHITE FRINGE: Red-billed gull, tarapunga, *Chroicocephalus scopulinus*

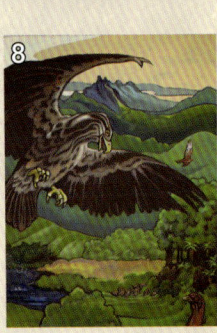

WINGS: Haast's eagle, pouakai, *Harpagornis moorei* (extinct). These enormous flying birds, the largest birds of prey in humankind's history, weighed up to 13 kilograms and had a wingspan of 3 metres. ▪ The common Australasian **harrier hawk**, kahu, *Circus approximans* is shown to scale with the eagle. ▪ The females of the **North Island giant moa**, *Dinornis novaezealandiae* (extinct) were the largest of these flightless birds – in fact they were among the largest birds in the world. ▪ **NZ swan**, *Cygnus sumnerensis* (extinct) ▪ **NZ stiff-tailed duck**, *Oxyura vantetsi* (extinct)

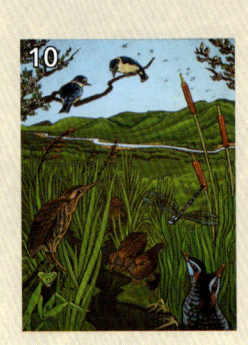

WETLANDS: The Waioeka River flows across floodplains to the sea. Protected behind stopbanks built during the 1960s, the plains are now used for dairying, maize, horticulture and crops.
▪ The **Australasian bittern**, matuku, *Botaurus poiciloptilus* is a shy bird, not often seen. It hides by remaining motionless with its head erect, to blend with the reeds of the marshland.
▪ **NZ praying mantis**, ro, *Orthodera novaezealandiae* is a predator. Its front legs have long sharp spines that are used as daggers to help kill its prey.
▪ When the **NZ giant bush dragonfly**, kapokapowai, *Uropetala carovei* is really hungry, it can devour up to 20 flies an hour. ▪ **NZ kingfisher**, kotare, *Halcyon sancta vagans* ▪ **NZ woodhen**, **weka**, *Gallirallus australis* ▪ **NZ banded rail**, mohopereu, *Rallus philippensis* ▪ Bullrush, **raupo**, *Typha orientalis* ▪ NZ tea-tree, **manuka**, *Leptospermum scoparium* ▪ It was to be another thousand years before humans arrived: they then used **NZ flax**, harakeke, *Phormium tenax* for weaving clothes, cloaks, baskets, mats, string and fishing nets.

RED SKIES: Saddleback, tieke, *Philesturnus carunculatus* was regarded as a guardian in Maori mythology. However, because they nest close to the ground, their young became vulnerable to (introduced) rats and stoats, and ironically, saddlebacks are now endangered and require protection. ▪ **Long-tailed bat**, pekapeka, *Chalinolobus tuberculatus* was thought by Maori to foretell death and disaster. ▪ **Fivefinger shrub**, puahou, *Pseudopanax arboreus*

GLORIOUS DAWN: Each of these birds has a particularly melodious song. North Island blue-wattled crow, **kokako**, *Callaeas cinerea* (endangered). The kokako's song is harmoniously rich; a pair will often sing a long, haunting, beautiful duet. ▪ **Bellbird**, korimako, *Anthornis melanura* is so named because it can sound like the chiming of bells, and must have reminded the European immigrants of their homelands far away. ▪ The song of the **grey warbler**, riroriro, *Gerygone igata* is a light and delicate trill. ▪ **Tui** is an enthusiastic vocalist, excellent mimic and a clever percussionist, using clicks and cackles, barks and wheezes. ▪ **Puriri** tree

16 BUGS FOR BREAKFAST: The **Huia**, *Heteralocha acutirostris* was hunted to extinction mainly because of its coveted tail feathers. ▪ NZ thrush, **Piopio**, *Turnagra capensis* (extinct) ▪ **Stitchbird**, hihi, *Notiomystis cincta* (endangered) ▪ **NZ fuchsia**, kotukutuku, konini, *Fuchsia excorticata* ▪ **Supplejack vine**, kareao ▪ **Hound's tongue fern**, kowaowao, *Microsorum pustulatus* ▪ **Lichens**, pukoko, *Stricta canariensis*

18 FLOWERS AND BERRIES: **NZ native pigeon**, kereru, *Hemiphaga novaeseelandiae* ▪ Red-crowned parakeet, **kakariki**, *Cyanoramphus novaeseelandiae* ▪ **Fantail**, piwakawaka, *Rhipidura fuliginosa* ▪ Trees of the genus *Vitex* are common throughout tropical and sub-tropical regions of the world, and many of them provide valuable timber, but **puriri**, *Vitex lucens* grows naturally only in New Zealand.

20 MIDNIGHT SNACK: **Kiwi**, *Apteryx mantelli* (endangered) ▪ **Morepork**, ruru, *Ninox novaeseelandiae* eating a moth ▪ **Laughing owl**, whekau (extinct) ▪ **Green gecko**, moko kakariki, *Naultinus elegans* is regarded by Maori as a bad omen ▪ **Greater short-tailed bat**, pekapeka, *Mystacina robusta* (extinct) ▪ **Lesser short-tailed bat**, pekapeka, *Mysticina tuberculata* (endangered) ▪ **Puriri moth**, pepetuna, *Aenetus virescens* ▪ **Large green cockchafer beetle**, tutaeruru, *Chlorochiton suturalis* ▪ **NZ glow-worm**, titiwai, *Arachnocampa luminosa* ▪ **Giant weta**, wetapunga, *Deinacrida heteracantha* is the heaviest insect in the world and can grow to the size of a rat. ▪ **NZ fuchsia**, kotukutuku, konini ▪ **Supplejack vine**, kareao

22 FALLEN GIANTS: The distinctive song of the migratory **shining cuckoo**, pipiwharauroa, *Chrysococcyx lucidus* announces the arrival of springtime; a new growing season. ▪ The **huhu beetle**, tunga rere does not eat and lives for only two weeks. The larvae, or huhu grub, lives in rotting wood. Apparently, if grilled, it has a taste similar to peanut butter. ▪ **NZ clematis** (in flower), puawhananga, *Clematis paniculata* ▪ NZ mahogany, **kohekohe** ▪ **Whiteywood**, mahoe, *Melicytus ramiflorus* ▪ **Hangehange**, *Geniostoma ligustrifolium* ▪ Perching lily, **kahakaha**, *Collospermum hastatum* ▪ **Kidney fern**, raurenga, *Trichomanes reniforme* ▪ **Brown toadstool fungi**, harore, of the genus *Pluteus* ▪ **Lichens**, pukoko, *Parmelia cuperata*, *Psoroma pholidotoides*

24 MIGRATION: A tribute to those mighty mariners who navigated the Pacific Ocean in twin-hulled canoes, using their knowledge of bird migration and the constellations of the night sky. ▪ **Long-tailed cuckoo**, koekoea, *Eudynamys taitensis*

26 LANDFALL: Legend has it that when Kupe first arrived in New Zealand, he thought there were people in the land because he heard voices – later identified to be the sounds of the kokako, the weka and the fantail. ▪ North Island blue-wattled crow, **kokako** (endangered) ▪ NZ woodhen, **weka** ▪ **Fantail**, piwakawaka ▪ **Pohutukawa** (in flower), *Metrosideros excelsa* ▪ **Pacific** or **Polynesian rat**, kiore, *Rattus exulans* ▪ Maori or Polynesian dog, **Kuri**, *Canis lupus familiaris* ▪ **Human**, *Homo sapiens*

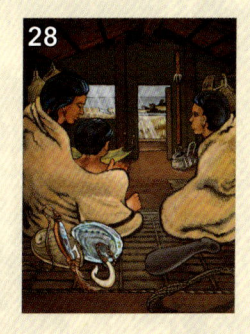

28 ADAPTATION: Polynesian settlers developed skills in gathering and growing food, and finding materials to make clothes, domestic items and houses. Cords and ropes were woven from the fibre of **NZ flax**. On the walls hang flax kete in reference to the legendary three kete of wisdom brought down to earth by the god Tane. ▪ Sedge, **pingao**, *Ficinia spiralis*. In spite of it being a 'cutty grass', pingao was often used by Maori for weaving into tukutuku panels because of its beautiful golden yellow colour once dried. ▪ Shell of the abalone, **rainbow paua**, *Haliotis iris*

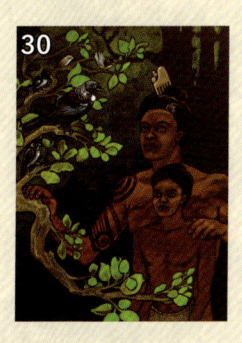

30 AWARENESS: In Maori legend, the four smaller birds are symbolic of exploration. When Maui went to search for and destroy the Goddess of Death, he chose piwakawaka, riroriro, miromiro and toutouwai as his companions on the journey. ▪ **Fantail**, piwakawaka ▪ **Grey warbler**, riroriro, nonoroheke, horirerire ▪ **Tit**, miromiro, *Petroica macrocephala* ▪ **North Island robin**, toutouwai, *Petroica australis longipes* ▪ **Tui** ▪ **NZ broadleaf**, kapuka, *Griselinia littoralis*

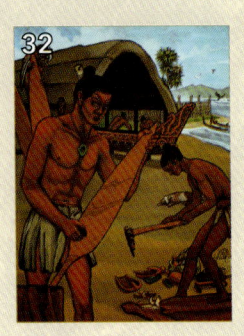

CRAFTSMANSHIP: The skills of the Maori settlers in using stone tools (and sometimes fire) to work with wood enabled them to create small implements, large meeting-houses and ornate war canoes. The neck-ornament is a greenstone poria – a carved ring used to secure captive birds. ▪ **Kaka**, *Nestor meridionalis* ▪ **Black-backed gull**, karoro, *Larus dominicanus dominicanus* ▪ **Southern right whale**, tohora, tohoraha, *Eubalaena australis* ▪ Maori or Polynesian dog, **Kuri** ▪ **Cabbage tree** (in flower), ti kouka, whanake, *Cordyline australis*. Tane's legendary three kete of wisdom, and binding cord woven from the fibre of **NZ flax**, harakeke.

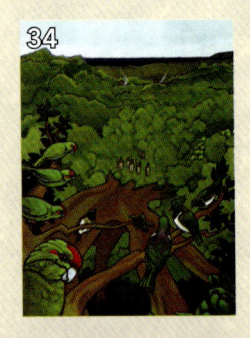

DISCOVERY: NZ native pigeon, kereru ▪ **Red-crowned parakeet, Kakariki** ▪ **Stitchbird**, hihi (endangered) ▪ **Puriri** trunk

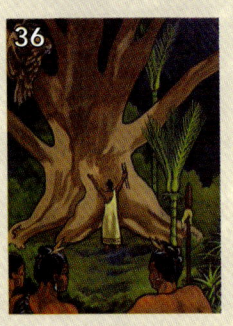

TAPU: The owl and lizard are symbolic of the tapu placed on Taketakerau. ▪ **Morepork**, ruru ▪ **Copper skink**, mokomoko, *Cyclodina aenea* ▪ **Puriri** trunk ▪ **Nikau palm** had many uses for Maori – the soft part of the inner leaves was eaten; also the young flower-clusters. Old, dried fronds made a waterproof thatch for buildings. ▪ **Kiekie**, *Freycinetia banksii*. Polynesian settlers ate the fruits of kiekie, and used the leaves for plaiting and weaving.

RITUAL: Morepork, ruru ▪ **Copper skink**, mokomoko ▪. The grub of the **puriri moth**, pepe tuna lives in a tree trunk for about five years and then emerges from a chrysalis as a moth that lives for only two days. ▪ **Puriri** trunk

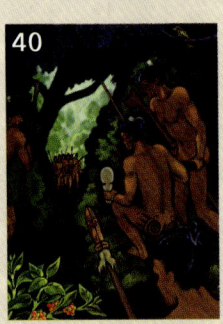

MARAUDERS: Bellbird, korimako ▪ **Supplejack vine**, kareao ▪ **Karamu**, *Coprosma robusta* – a healing plant for wounds; also used by priests to ritually sprinkle warriors who were going into battle

ENDEAVOUR: Although most of the creatures in this picture are watching the ship, the morepork and gecko are looking at each other … ▪ **Morepork**, ruru ▪ **Bellbird**, korimako ▪ **NZ native pigeon**, kereru ▪ **Green gecko**, moko kakariki ▪ **Nikau palm** ▪ **Black tree fern, Ponga**, mamaku, *Cyathea medullaris* ▪ **Leather-leaf fern**, ngarara wehi, *Pyrrosia eleagnifolia* ▪ **Puriri** ▪ White Island, Whakaari is an active volcano 40 km off the coastline of the Bay of Plenty.

WHALERS: ▪ **Long-finned pilot whale** (blackfish), upokohue, parakipihi, *Globicephala melas* ▪ **Ship** or **black rat**, pouhawaiki, *Rattus rattus*

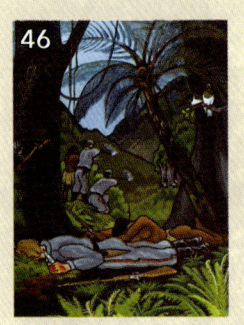

LAND WARS: Fantail, piwakawaka ▪ **NZ native pigeon**, kereru ▪ **Miro** tree trunk, *Prumnopitys ferruginea* ▪ **Pukatea** tree trunk – note the fan-like buttresses ▪ **Black tree fern, Ponga**, mamaku ▪ **Crown fern**, kiokio, *Blechnum discolor* ▪ **Supplejack vine**, kareao ▪ **Lichen**, pukoko, *Peltigera sp.* ▪ Uniform of the NZ Forest Rangers ▪ Enfield 1853 rifle-musket

WASHDAY: A tribute to the pioneer women who laboured long and hard to care for their families; their living conditions being quite different from the comforts of the Old Country. ▪ **Cow**, kau, *Bos taurus* ▪ **Cat**, ngeru, poti, puihi, *Felis domesticus*

TARAWERA ASH: Mirage of the gaping cleft of Mount Tarawera, the ash of which extended over 65 km to reach the forest where Taketakerau stands. Mirage of 'Waka Wairua', the phantom canoe seen crossing Lake Tarawera ten days before the eruption. ▪ **Tuatara**, *Sphenodon punctatus* – regarded as a messenger of Whiro, the god of death and disaster. Given the magnitude of this disaster, the tuatara (a reptile that has remained almost the same for 200 million years) stands in for the lizard as a symbol of the tapu for this illustration. ▪ **Morepork**, ruru

52 SACRED BONES: Morepork, ruru ▪ **Forest gecko**, moko pirirakau, *Hoplodactylus granulatus* ▪ **Horse**, hoiho, *Equus* ▪ Sap-eating **elephant weevil**, *Rhyncodes ursus* ▪ **Nikau palm** ▪ The barbed **bush lawyer** vine, tataramoa, *Rubus schmidelioides* ▪ **Puriri**

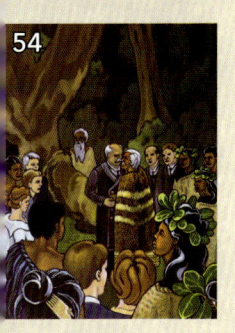

54 MANA AND MYSTIQUE: We do not know exactly where New Zealand's prime minister was on this particular day, but the artist's interpretation of this event has placed William Massey here. He wears a formal frock-coat. The chief wears a ceremonial kiwi-feather cloak with taniko border. The Maori women are wearing korowai cloaks woven from the fibre of **NZ flax**, harakeke, and chaplets made from **karaka** leaves (*Corynocarpus laevigatus*). The man on the right could be Norman Potts, who would have been in his late 30s. ▪ **Puriri**

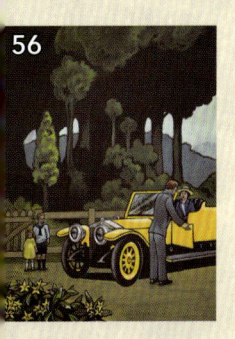

56 OPEN GATE: Corokia, korokio, *Corokia buddleioides* ▪ **NZ honeysuckle, Rewarewa**, *Knightia excelsa* ▪ Rolls-Royce Silver Ghost 1906–26

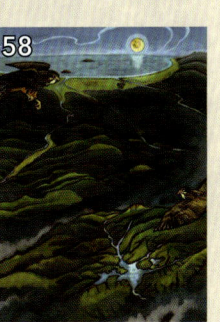

58 ABOVE THE MISTS: NZ falcon (male and female), sparrowhawk, karearea, *Falco novaeseelandiae* – the male has his talons out to display the orange under-parts and legs. Falcons can sky-dive for live prey at almost 200 km/hr. ▪ Whale Island, Moutohora ▪ White Island, Whakaari ▪ Whakatane River ▪ Waimana River ▪ Waioeka River ▪ Otara/Pakihi River ▪ Lake Waikaremoana ▪ Te Urewera National Park ▪ Taketakerau

60 PRIMARY PRODUCTION: Sheep, *Ovis aries* ▪ The **border collie dog,** *Canis lupus familiaris* – developed from dogs used along the borders of Scotland and England, which in turn, had apparently descended from dogs used by the Vikings to herd reindeer; a very energetic breed, it loves to work. ▪ **Cow**, kau ▪ **Foxglove**, *Digitalis purpurea* ▪ **Tawa**, *Beilschmiedia tawa* ▪ 'Fletcher' top-dressing aeroplane – a NZ innovation ▪ Waioeka River ▪ State Highway 2

62 EXTINCTION: Laughing owl, whekau (extinct 1914) ▪ **Haast's eagle**, pouakai, hokioi (extinct 1300–1400) ▪ **North Island giant moa** (representing 14 species, all extinct 1300–1400) ▪ **North Island goose**, *Cnemiornis gracilis* (representing two species, both extinct 1300–1400) ▪ **NZ swan** (extinct) ▪ **Huia** (extinct 1907) ▪ **NZ thrush**, piopio (representing two species, both extinct by 1905) ▪ **NZ wren**, *Acanthisittidae* (there were six species; four of which became extinct 1888–1972).

64 ENDURANCE: Pepper tree, **kawakawa**, *Macropiper excelsum* is a plant with many healing properties. ▪ **Kawakawa looper moth**, *Cleora scriptaria* – the caterpillars of which are responsible for the shot-holes commonly seen in kawakawa leaves.

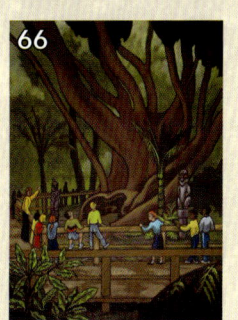

66 RESPECT: The two wooden statues are guardians of Taketakerau. They are called tekoteko (carved human forms). **Lemonwood**, tarata, *Pittosporum eugenioides* ▪ **King fern**, para, *Ptisana salicina* (formerly *Marattia salicina*) ▪ Groundcover, **NZ begonia**, parataniwha, *Elatostema rugosum* ▪ **Nikau palm** ▪ Taketakerau

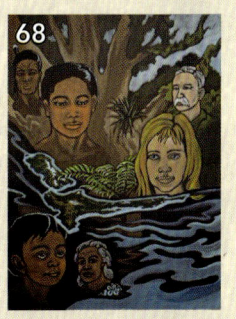

68 HERITAGE: The **silver fern**, kaponga, ponga, *Cyathea dealbata* was first trademarked as a New Zealand icon in 1885. ▪ Perching lily, **kahakaha** ▪ **Puriri**

74 SOVEREIGN: Red admiral butterfly, kahukura, *Bassaris gonerilla* (formerly *Vanessa gonerilla*). The Maori name means 'red cloak'. The name also appears in Maori mythology as the god of travellers; of life, death and disease. Red Admirals are strong and long-lived – up to nine months, at the end of which they may be quite battered and worn – just like Taketakerau. ▪ **Nikau palm** ▪ **King fern**, para

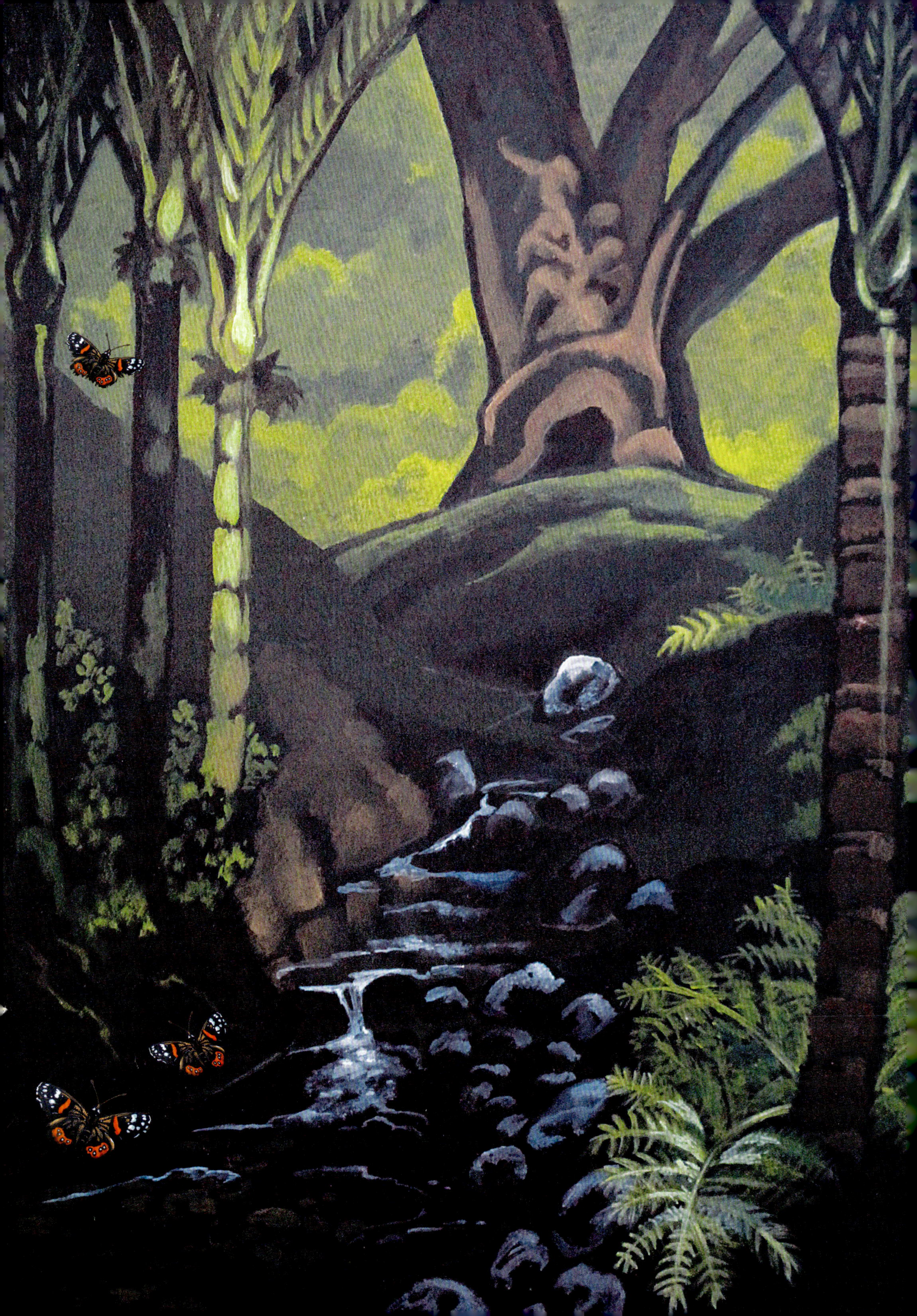

Taketakerau still reigns over a large and varied collection of native flora that includes many fine puriri specimens in the Hukutaia Domain, ten kilometres inland from the town of Opotiki, in the Eastern Bay of Plenty, New Zealand.

The wide variety of native plants that enhance the natural bush of the Hukutaia Domain are there mainly because of the horticultural skills, dedication and enthusiasm freely given by an energetic supporter – Norman Potts, an Opotiki solicitor. A highly regarded amateur botanist, he spent over 30 years collecting plants and seeds from all around the country, which he then introduced to the Domain, now making it one of the best public collections of New Zealand native plants. When Norman Potts died in 1970 at the age of 84, the community built a stone wall and seat at the entrance gates as a tribute to his love of the Domain, the plants and people of Opotiki.

Visit **www.themillenniumtree.com** for more about the author, the artists and the tree.

Thanks to Patricia Howitt for her striking illustrations and Kelly Spencer for her superb pen and ink drawings. Thanks also to Eliza Bartlett, Murray Darroch, Colin Bassett and Mark Anstis. Thanks to Random House – Knopf for permission to use the quote on the title page from *Timeline*, by Michael Crichton. I am especially grateful to Dorothy Fabish and Mildred Burton. I very much appreciated the advice and direction given by local identities, iwi, and educationalists (especially Woodlands School and Opotiki Primary School). Thanks also to the many friends who over the years have cheered me on. And extra special thanks and appreciation to Peter and the boys for all their love, encouragement and support.

National Library of New Zealand Cataloguing-in-Publication Data
Anstis, Marnie.
Taketakerau : the Millennium Tree / Marnie Anstis ; illustrated by Patricia Howitt.
ISBN 978-1-877577-68-0
1. Historic trees—New Zealand—Juvenile literature. 2. World history—
Juvenile literature. 3. New Zealand—History—Juvenile literature.
[1. Historic trees. 2. World history. 3. New Zealand—History.]
[1. Pūriri. reo 2. Kōrero nehe. reo]
I. Howitt, Patricia. II. Title.
NZ993—dc 22

Concept and text © Marnie Anstis

Painted illustrations © Patricia Howitt

Drawings © Kelly Spencer

Production by Matthew Bartlett, Steele Roberts Aotearoa

Published by

Marnie Anstis
Woodlands Road
Opotiki, New Zealand
millennium@anstis.co.nz

in association with

Steele Roberts Aotearoa
Box 9321, Wellington
New Zealand
www.steeleroberts.co.nz